January

Apple

In 1732 the Kensington nurseryman, Robert Furber, published *The Twelve Months of Fruit*, a set of engravings from oil paintings by Pieter Casteels who was also the artist for Furber's earlier work, *The Twelve Months of Flowers*. Under each plate is a key listing the name of the fruit shown, together with, 'what trees are proper for standards, dwarfs or espaliers' (first, second and third columns respectively). The fourth column shows the 'aspect they require by the initial letter of the four cardinal points, East, West, North and South'.

There are thousands of varieties of the apple, which is a member of the rose family and the genus *Malus*. Its history is difficult to trace as trees may have been cultivated since the stone age. A writer in AD 4 named thirty-seven varieties. Before improvements in transportation, the apple was the only fresh fruit in winter and great effort was put into improving the familiar crab-apple of the hedgerow, and developing cultivars specifically for eating, cooking or cider-making.

By the start of the seventeenth century, settlers were taking apples with them to America and from then on to all other suitable parts of the world. Furber lists ninety-five apples, among them the Golden Pippin, a much appreciated dessert apple in the sixteenth and seventeenth centuries, and the Golden Reinette which was known before 1650 and is still grown in Europe to this day.

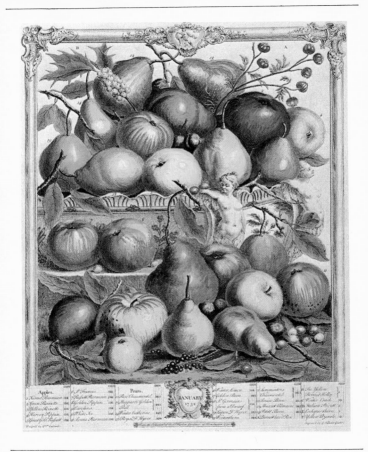

JANUARY
1732

3

Apple and Celery Soup

Serves 4

2oz (50g) butter
2tbs (30ml) sunflower oil
4 stalks celery with leaves
  sliced
1 medium onion sliced
1 carrot sliced

6 eating apples
1pt (600ml) good chicken or
  beef stock
a pinch or grating of nutmeg
salt and freshly ground pepper
finely chopped parsley

Heat 1oz (25g) of the butter and the oil in a large saucepan. Add the celery, onion and carrot and stir for a few minutes. Slice 5 of the apples, including the peel and core and add to the vegetables. Cook together stirring for a few more minutes. Next add the stock and simmer covered for 15 minutes. Strain or pass through a sieve and season with the nutmeg, salt and pepper. Before reheating and serving the soup, peel, core and slice the remaining apple and fry in the butter until the slices are soft and golden. Garnish the hot soup with the apple slices and a sprinkling of parsley.

The Gravenstien Apple.

February

Juniper

In February, Furber list an apple called Old Wife which appears to have wrinkled skin, and a double-flowering pear, 'like other pear trees except that it blossoms twice a year . . . at Christmas, and in the Spring'. On almost every plate Furber lists 'some uncommon fruits, which are beautiful to the eye, but unfit for eating'. And it is in this category that he places the decorative Turkey juniper.

There are over sixty species, all of which belong to the Cypress family, but the only one native to England is *Juniperus communis*. The common juniper grows wild throughout Europe, Asia and North America and likes high altitudes of up to 8000 feet. Junipers are shrubs or small evergreen trees with pointed leaves that have a white band on their upper surface, and the male and female plants are usually separate. The male has small yellow cones and the female has dark red or blue fruits which only fully ripen in their second season.

Oil of juniper, acquired by distillation, has been used for hundreds of years because of its diuretic properties, and in Lapland the bark is used to make rope. The berries are used for flavouring gin and other drinks. The French for juniper is *genièvre* from which gin derives its name.

March

Almond

As a Kensington gardener, Furber was fortunate in being able to take advantage of southern England's mild climate for growing more sensitive species. It is certainly curious to see olives and Furber recommends them, 'the sort represented in the plate is that which is call'd the Luca olive, which I have had bring ripe fruit fit to make oil of'.

Two sorts of almond are pictured, the great almond and the soft almond. Although they are no longer known by these names they are almost certainly *Prunus dulcis var. dulcis,* the sweet almond and *Prunus dulcis var. amara*, the bitter almond, respectively. The sweet almond is edible and is used by bakers, confectioners and consumers. More of this nut is sold on the world markets than any other species. The oil of the bitter almond is used for flavouring and skin cosmetics, but the kernel and untreated oil are extremely bitter to taste, containing a poison, prussic or hydrocyanic acid.

The tree, a native to western Asia and Morocco, is very similar to the peach with its early pink flowers. Festivals honoured the beautiful almond blossom, and before electricity, firepots were placed in the almond groves ready to be lit if a frost threatened. The fruit is usually much smaller than that of the peach and is green with a leathery texture. The ripe fruit splits open to reveal the stone which in turn contains the valuable almond kernel.

Almond Biscuits   makes about 38 2½in (6.3cm) biscuits

3oz (75g) almonds blanched
3½oz (100g) sugar
2oz (50g) unsalted butter
  softened
pinch of salt

2tbs (30ml) double cream
2 egg whites from size 4 eggs
1oz (25g) plain flour
1tbs (15ml) rum

Finely grind 2oz (50g) of the almonds with the sugar in a liquidizer or processor. Roughly chop the remaining almonds and set aside.

Preheat the oven to Gas Mark 7/425°F/220°C. Cream the butter with the sugar mixture, salt and cream. Add the egg whites, stirring only enough to blend. Sift the flour and fold in carefully, then stir in the rum. Spoon the mixture a teaspoon at a time on to a well greased baking sheet and flatten with the back of a spoon. Sprinkle with the reserved nuts and bake for 5 minutes, or until the edges are beginning to go brown. Remove from the oven and allow to stand a minute or two before removing with a spatula. If they become too brittle to remove easily, reheat them in the oven with the door open for a few seconds. Curl on a rolling pin until firm. Store when cool in an airtight container.

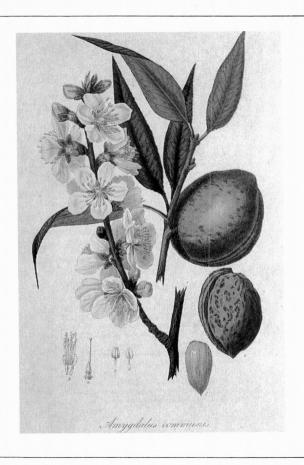

Amygdalus communis.

April

Seville Orange

According to Furber the seville orange 'is a noted tree of the greenhouse, and makes the pleasantest plant of all the oranges. Set this plant in the greenhouse in September, and bring it out in May, according to the old rule, when the Mulberry leaf is as large as a crows foot, for then you may be sure the weather is settled.'

Almost all citrus fruits originated from China and south east Asia. The flowers, leaves and fruit skins of all the species have essential oils which are sometimes extracted for use in perfumes and other toiletries.

The seville, sour or bitter orange, *Citrus aurantium*, has fruit so sour that it is practically inedible unless cooked, but it is used for making marmalade of which Britain has the highest consumption in the world. The fruit is 2¾–3½ inches across, is usually spherical but sometimes flattened at one or both ends, and its core is hollow when ripe. It was introduced to Spain by the Arabs who brought it from Asia and is still grown there today to supply the British market.

It is the hardiest of all the oranges and for this reason was used as a rootstock for grafting until it was discovered that it was susceptible to *Tristeza*, a citrus disease. Perhaps this hardiness also explains why it was widely cultivated in England. Orangeries were built to protect the plants from frost and when the weather was 'settled' the trees, in tubs on wheels, were rolled outside for the summer.

Seville Orange Ratafia

Makes 1qt (1.1litre)

6 seville oranges
18oz (500g) sugar
1 stick cinnamon

2tsp (10ml) coriander seeds
1qt (1.1litre) eau de vie or gin

Peel the oranges without the pith and chop finely. Squeeze the juice into a large glass jar or bottle. Add the sugar, chopped rind and spices. Pour on the spirits, seal and leave to infuse for 2 months. Filter the ratafia and bottle.

P. Tofani dis...   *Guer. Pera inc...*

CITRUS AURANTIUM Striatum

Arancia Scannellata

May

Strawberry

The strawberry, *Fragaria species*, is one of the 'youngest' fruits grown today. The familiar berries we know have only been available since the early nineteenth century. Furber's plate shows earlier and smaller varieties: the wood or alpine strawberry, *F. vesca*, fairly common in woods in the northern hemisphere, has been grown in gardens since the Middle Ages when it was found that it would produce fruit twice as large if well-cared for. Even so, the delicious fruit is very small and tedious to collect. The little scarlet or scarlet woodland strawberry, *F. virginiana*, was introduced to France in 1624 from eastern America and taken to England in 1629. It is still grown today.

Francois Frézier (from which comes the French, *fraisier*), found some strawberry plants while he was spying in Chile in 1714. He sent some back to France but only five survived the six months' journey, and once established, these flowered but would not fruit, because the male and female plants are separate and Frézier's plants were all female. This was the west coast pine strawberry, *F. chloensis*, which grows all along the Pacific and has pale fruit which taste like pineapple.

The American species, *F. virginiana*, was geographically isolated by the Rockies, but when hybridized with Frézier's plants gave much larger fruit. By 1800 the first of these hybrids was on the market, but only one variety, Laxton's Royal Sovereign (1892) is still grown today.

Coeurs de Crème aux Fraises   Serves 4–6

2lb (900g) low fat yoghurt   3 small egg whites
3½oz (100g) castor sugar   8oz (225g) strawberries

Ideally small heart-shaped moulds with holes in the base
for drainage should be used for this cream, but small
ramekins can be substituted.

Drain the yoghurt over two layers of muslin over-
night. The next day turn the yoghurt out into a bowl and
stir in the sugar. Beat the egg whites until stiff, but not
dry, and fold into the yoghurt. Line the bases of the
individual moulds with a layer of kitchen towel. Spoon in
the cream, and place the moulds on a dish in the
refrigerator to continue draining.

To serve; slip a knife around the edge of the moulds,
turn out onto a serving dish and remove the paper. Serve
surrounded with strawberries.

June

Gooseberry

In May twelve kinds of apples are listed and in June there are four, which at first sight is a little confusing since most people think of apples as autumn or winter fruit. In fact there are still varieties today that may be picked in spring or early summer. The fruit simply remains on the tree all winter and will stay reasonably hard throughout. This is what led to names such as Longhanger and Warner's Long Keeping Pippin.

June is really soft fruit season and thirteen varieties of gooseberry are listed. The gooseberry, *Ribes grossularia*, is also known as the catberry and is closely related to the currant except that it is spiny. The plant naturalized in many parts of Europe and probably originated in North Africa. It has been cultivated for centuries and was extremely popular because the berries could be eaten while young or when fully ripe.

In the 1800s there were many gooseberry clubs in the Midlands. People tried to grow the biggest possible single fruit and special scales were designed to weigh the minute differences. The Royal Horticultural Society listed 400 cultivars which could be categorized according to hairy fruit, non-hairy, green, white, yellow or red berries as well as shape, size, flavour or growth habit of the bush. The gooseberry is less popular now, possibly because it is susceptible to mildew, it has spines and it is a host to a fungus that attacks white pine trees.

JUNE
1732

Gooseberry Sauce

Top and tail the gooseberries, place in a saucepan and barely cover with cold water. Simmer very gently until the berries are just tender. Drain carefully, return to the pan and add a good knob of butter and a pinch of ginger. Serve the sauce hot as an accompaniment for mackerel.

Gooseberry and Elderflower Jam   Makes 5lb (2.25kg)

10 heads of elderflowers
3lb (1.4kg) green gooseberries
  slightly underripe

2pt (1.1litre) water
3lb (1.4kg) sugar

Cut off the stems of the elderflowers close to the flowers and tie in a muslin bag. Top and tail the gooseberries and put into a preserving pan with the water and elderflowers. Simmer gently for 30 minutes, until the fruit is very soft, stirring occasionally to prevent sticking. Remove the elderflowers, add the sugar and stir until dissolved. Boil rapidly until setting point is reached. Pot and cover.

Verte commune.

De l'Imprimerie de Langlois

July

Peach

Peaches were grown for their beautiful blossoms as well as for their luxurious taste. Furber describes the double-blossomed peach, 'this makes one of the prettiest trees I have seen ... and as it blows early, should be placed in wildernesses among other flowering trees or shrubs'.

The peach, *Prunus persica*, is a small tree which has a fairly short life span of twenty to twenty-five years and is a member of the rose family. Its scientific name comes from the belief that it originated in Persia as Iran was then known. In fact it comes from China where there are records of it from 551 BC.

In Europe it has been known since before the first century BC, when Alexander the Great possibly brought it to the Graeco-Roman world. The modern varieties are very similar to those of the Romans and Chinese, as can be seen in ancient frescos.

The Spanish took the peach to South America in the sixteenth century and a hundred years later they were being grown in California. By the nineteenth century the fruit was flourishing in Australia.

Britain has known the peach since the Anglo-Saxons who gave it the name of 'perseoc-treou', and by the time of Elizabeth I they were in cultivation. British gardeners have produced many splendid varieties, one of which, Pitmaston Orange, raised in 1815 by Mr Edwards of Pitmaston is still unsurpassed in flavour.

JULY
1732

Spiced Peaches   Makes 5lb (2.2kg)

2lb (900g) sugar   1tsp (5ml) allspice berries
1pt (600ml) cider vinegar   4 blades mace
1 stick cinnamon   1in (2.5cm) piece fresh ginger
6 cloves   4lb (1.75kg) peaches

Dissolve the sugar in the vinegar over a low heat. Peel and
chop the ginger and add it with the other spices to the
vinegar. Peel the peaches by dropping them into boiling
water for a few seconds. If the peaches are large, halve
them. Drop them into the boiling vinegar syrup and
simmer gently until they are just tender. Lift them out
carefully and put into hot sterilized jars. Boil the syrup to
reduce it slightly and pour over the peaches, dividing the
spices between the jars. Seal and store for 2–3 months
before using.

Pavie de Pompone.

August

Apricot

Only the affluent could afford gardeners capable of producing peaches and nectarines and other delicacies. Indeed Furber dedicated his *Short Introduction to Gardening* to his subscribers who included the Duke of Atholl, the Duchess of Bolton, Sir Orlando Bridgman and William Hippifly.

The apricot, *Prunus armeniaca*, has a similar history to the peach. It originated in China where it has been known for at least 4000 years and then spread to the Far East and the Mediterranean. There are wild apricots throughout temperate zones including Africa and these Hunza apricots are surrounded by myths of giving everlasting youth. The apricot tree is sturdier than the peach, growing twenty to thirty feet high with white or pink flowers and fruit that varies in depth of colouring, size, flavour and tenderness.

By 1570 the apricot was also grown in many northern gardens as it was found to fruit fairly well in colder climates, because it must have some chilling in its dormant stage. As people emigrated from Europe it was dispersed further, always growing best in climates similar to that of China. By the eighteenth century *Prunus armeniaca* was growing in America, South Africa, New Zealand and Australia.

In 1760 Lord Anson planted an apricot stone that became a famous late-flowering variety, while Miss Shipley of Blenheim, England, raised Shipley's Blenheim in the early 1800s which is still grown in California.

Apricock		Roman		Noblsse		Plumbs		Blue Perdrigon		Pears	
1 Brussels		7 Peas		14 Chancelor		1 Royal Dolphin		21 Peach Carpenter		27 Barbou	
Grapes		8 Portugal		15 Nivette		2 Matchless		22 Chaton		28 Vadow Hore	
2 White Sweet Water		9 Small Scarlet		16 Royal George		3 Prune Royall		23 Sennegall		29 Black Wallberry	
3 Black Sweet Water		10 Italian		17 Marquard		4 Catherinehall		24 Black Damascen		30 The Apple Pear	
Nectarines		11 Argile		18 Double Jardin		5 Lobert		25 Chinas Nordens		31 The Musk Palace	
4 Vaningston		Peaches		19 Mountaigners		6 Smith Windsor		26 Mino Claud		32 The Thornmann	
5 Marly small		12 Persique		20 St Lawrence		6 Rotfeld Clous		Rain Claud		33 Mushull	

AUGUST
1732

September

Plum

Plums have been grown and gathered for centuries. Many species grow wild in the northern hemisphere such as the sloe, bullace, damson and gage but most of the modern cultivars, *Prunus domestica*, came from hybridizing the sloe, *Prunus spinosa*, with a western Asian species, *P. cerasifera*. These hybrids have further been selected for dessert, cooking and drying plums.

The sloe is small and sour and is used for sloe gin and wine. The bullace, although milder than the sloe, is still not very good. The damson originated in Damascus and ripens six weeks before the bullace, giving a sweeter, richer fruit which is excellent for jam.

The gage, *Prunus italica*, may have been in cultivation earlier, but was certainly introduced into England from France in 1725. They say that Sir Thomas Gage lost the labels on the trees which he brought across the Channel and, forgetting their French name of Reine Claude he gave the plant his own name. Later it became known as the greengage. Furber in fact uses the correct name and does not honour Gage with the trees' discovery.

As many of the best plums originated in hedgerows, their parentage can never be precisely known. The Victoria plum, first found in a Sussex wood in 1840, is self-fertile and a reliable cropper which is why it is grown so much commercially.

35

Plum Iced Soufflé   Serves 4

8oz (225g) stewed damson
  plums
1tbs (15ml) armagnac or
  brandy

3½oz (100g) sugar
5tbs (75ml) water
2 egg whites
¼pt (150ml) double cream

Wrap a collar around a 1pt (600ml) soufflé dish or 4 individual ones. Purée and strain the plums. Dissolve the sugar in the water over a low heat in a heavy-bottomed saucepan. Bring to the boil and boil to the soft-ball stage, 239°F/115°C on a sugar thermometer. Beat the egg whites until stiff, then slowly pour the hot syrup on to the egg whites while continuing to beat. Beat until the mixture is very stiff and has cooled. Whip the cream and fold in to the mixture, then fold in the plum purée. Spoon into the prepared dish and freeze. Allow to soften in a refrigerator for 2 hours before removing the collar and serving.

PRUSUS DOMESTICA Claudiana

Susina della Regina Claudia

October

Pineapple

The pineapple, *Ananas comosus*, originated in South America where *ananas* means pine-like, and *comosus*, tufted. It is an easy plant to grow in the right temperature and once discovered, it was quickly distributed world-wide and has even become naturalized in parts of Asia and Africa.

Columbus was said to have taken the pineapple to Spain, and in 1583 the Portuguese took it to India. In the late seventeenth century it was brought to England and grown widely in private and commercial hothouses. A pineapple craze started and Mr William Speechley had 10,000 plants in pots for the Duke of Portland. They were used to surprise guests and quickly became a symbol of hospitality. Stone pineapples were placed on the columns of stately homes around the countryside. As one can see from Furber's plate the pineapples grown then were much smaller than those of today. The Queen produces 2–3lb fruit and is still cultivated in South Africa. In 1841, however, the much larger Cayenne or Kew Giant was introduced and quickly became the most widely grown variety. The main problem with pineapples is the sharp, spiny leaves which are unpopular, and so a smooth Cayenne with less flavour and no spines is gradually superseding the time-honoured Kew Giant.

Apples						Luclatian Bitters			Catherine			Sheldon	
Red Streak		Black Hamburgh		White Frontiniac		Peaches			Pears			Imperatrice Plumb	
Quince-de-Portugal		St Piere		Royal black		of Egyptian			Parus du Roy			Fig Apple	
Cherries		Red Frontiniac		Muscol Frontiniac		Luculian Hermit-fr			Autumn Pear			Balsam Apricot	
Cornelian		Corinth without Stone		White Frontiniac		of Berchesk			La Marquise			Sweet Almond	
Morello		Red Hamburg		Medlars		Fruits Florentine			Autumn Colmar			Red Barberry	
Grapes		Brick coloured		English		from a Standart			Swiss 199			White Barberry	

OCTOBER
1730

From the Collection of her Grace the Dutchess of Beaumont 1732

Design'd by Mr Furbes.   Engrav'd by H Fletcher

39

Chicken Livers with Pineapple · Serves 4

1lb (450g) chicken livers
6tbs (90ml) sunflower oil
6oz (175g) fresh or canned
   pineapple in chunks
2oz (50g) blanched almonds
½pt (300ml) pineapple juice

4tbs (60ml) cider vinegar
½oz (15g) sugar
1tbs (15ml) soya sauce
½oz (15g) cornstarch or
   arrowroot
salt and ground black pepper

Cut the chicken livers in half and remove any fat or discoloured pieces. Dry on kitchen towel. Heat the oil in a frying pan and sauté the livers until they are brown on the outside but the insides are still pink. Season well with salt and pepper and add the pineapple chunks and the almonds. Cook together for a few minutes then remove the pan from the heat. Cover to keep warm while you prepare the sauce.

Combine the pineapple juice, vinegar, sugar, soya sauce and cornstarch in a saucepan and stir over low heat until thickened. Pour over the chicken livers and serve at once. Rice and stir-fry vegetables go well with this dish.

November

Grapes

Furber's Restling or Remish grape is undoubtedly today's Riesling, a term used to describe the pale wine grapes grown around the Rhine valley. There are many different kinds of grapevines but the species that produces the most palatable fruits is *Vitis vinifera*, which yields dessert grapes, wine, currants and raisins. The species probably originated in Caucasian areas but also grows wild in western Asia. It is one of the oldest cultivated plants, known by the Egyptians over 6000 years ago.

The Greeks and Romans refined viticulture and introduced it to their colonies such as Britain, which received the grape in AD 10, where it flourished in certain areas until the fourteenth century when competition from France and a possible climatic change led to a decline. The closing of the monasteries in the sixteenth century also resulted in fewer vines but some vineyards continued into the eighteenth century and Furber certainly has illustrated a large number of varieties.

Viticulture was boosted again by the invention of hothouses, but in the middle of the nineteenth century, phylloxera threatened to kill all the vines, and the cultivars were only saved by grafting them to resistant American root-stocks.

Furber illustrates the Black Hamburg, a superlative vine for the cold greenhouse, a variety of which still grows today at Hampton Court where it was planted in 1769.

Casserole of Pheasant with grapes

Serves 4

1 pheasant with the liver
4oz (100g) clarified butter
1 onion chopped
1 carrot chopped
¼pt (150ml) white wine
¼pt (150ml) game stock

¼pt (150ml) double cream
5tbs (75ml) cognac
4 triangles bread
salt and freshly ground pepper
1lb (450g) white grapes pipped

Preheat oven to Gas Mark 4/350°F/180°C. Lightly brown the pheasant with the onion and carrot in 2oz (50g) of the butter. Cover the pheasant with greaseproof paper and the lid and roast in the oven for 45 minutes. Meanwhile fry the bread in 1½oz (35g) of butter until golden. Remove to kitchen towelling. Add the liver to the pan with the remaining butter and cook until brown mashing it up with a fork. Season well with salt and pepper. Spread on the bread and keep warm. When the bird is cooked remove it from the casserole and keep warm. Deglaze the casserole with the wine and stock, and reduce by half. Add the cream and the cognac flamed in a ladle. Season with salt and pepper. Strain into a saucepan, add the grapes and simmer for a few minutes to heat the grapes. Serve the carved pheasant on the toast coated with the sauce.

LEPIDOPTERA *Sphinx.*
HYMENOPTERA *Vespa.*

PL.VIII.

ELPENOR *Sphinx Lin. Syst. Nat. 541. Habit in* VITIS *Vitis alba*
TRAPA *spatiosa Habit in Europa.* (*Gegebenwetzt*) *Habit in Europa.* *Mth. Dissol. Brit.*

Drawn & Engraved & Publish'd by I. Mill----n --London --Little Covent Garden according to the Catalogue 1773.

December

Pear

In the Christmas month of December Furber has two kinds of grapes, the white and red raisins, which were obviously suitable for drying to provide for the winter months when other fruit was sparse. The only fruit Furber lists for every month of the year is the pear, *Pyrus communis*. There are over thirty species of pear from very different climatic areas, but the European wild pear, *P. communis*, is a native of all temperate Europe and Asia.

The fruit has been grown since ancient times and Pliny mentioned thirty-nine varieties known to the Romans. By the sixteenth century 232 varieties were listed and today there are over three thousand. Pears like a warm summer with sufficient rainfall and are grown mainly in France, Belgium and West Germany. They are used for dessert, cooking and perry, for which the cultivars have remained basically unchanged for over 2500 years.

French varieties such as the seventeenth-century Jargonelle, shown in July's plate, had for long been grown in England. By the eighteenth and nineteenth centuries English gardeners were breeding their own varieties of which the two best known are John William's Bon Chrétien (known as the Bartlett pear in America following a Gage-like incident crossing the Atlantic) and Thomas River's Conference, both of which are still grown. The French Doyenné du Comice was bred in 1849 and is perhaps one of the finest-tasting pears grown today.